blue
rider
press

# Horace

*&*

# Agnes

# Horace
## ✫ & ✫
# Agnes
·······································
## A Love Story

### Lynn Dowling
### & Asia Kepka

BLUE RIDER PRESS · NEW YORK

blue
rider
press

An imprint of Penguin Random House LLC
375 Hudson Street
New York, New York 10014

Photographs on pages 154 (middle) and 155 (bottom left)
are used with permission of Jeanne F. Ramalho.

Library of Congress Cataloging-in-Publication Data
Names: Dowling, Lynn, author. | Kepka, Asia, photographer.
Title: Horace and Agnes : a love story | Lynn Dowling and Asia Kepka.
Description: New York : Blue Rider Press, 2016.
Identifiers: LCCN 2016016475 | ISBN 9780399575495 (hardback)
Subjects: LCSH: Photography, Humorous. | Photobooks. | Groomsby, Horace
(Fictitious character) | Groomsby, Agnes (Fictitious character) |
BISAC: HUMOR / General.
Classification: LCC TR679.5.D69    2016 | DDC 770—dc23
LC record available at
https://lccn.loc.gov/2016016475

Printed in China
1   3   5   7   9   10   8   6   4   2

*Book design by Lauren Kolm*
*Cover photographs by Asia Kepka*
*Cover lettering by Siobhan Gallagher*
*Cover design by Jason Booher*

To Paula Tognarelli, who saw the love early
and propelled us to the next level.

Love takes off masks that we fear we cannot live without
and know we cannot live within.

—*James Baldwin*

Twenty years ago, Horace Groomsby met Agnes on a train. It was overcrowded and stiflingly hot. Horace politely asked if he could possibly take the last remaining seat next to Agnes. She moved her pocketbook onto her lap and smiled. He gently slid into his seat and smiled back. She was shy at first, but Horace enthusiastically engaged her in conversation. They talked for more than two hours. So engrossed with each other, they both missed their stops.

LOVE IS BLIND

During the summer months, Agnes and Horace enjoy lounging on the davenport singing their favorite Bobby Vinton tunes. Agnes has an exquisite voice. Horace should probably avoid singing, but he plays the accordion so poorly that he drowns out his own voice. It wouldn't matter to Agnes anyway. She loves listening to Horace no matter what.

ACCORDION

Agnes makes Horace's lunch every workday. Horace pleads with her not to, but there she is, every morning, handing it to him with a big grin. "I hope it's not egg salad," he says as he grasps the handle of his lunch pail. "You know it is," she says before she kisses him. Horace despises egg salad and Agnes never makes it for him; it's just their morning ritual.

RITUALS

*H*orace fancies himself a yardman, but the grass barely grows. Agnes has already made her peace that she will never be the owner of a beautiful lawn, but she still brings Horace lemonade while he rigorously manicures the remaining few blades.

Agnes is determined to go on a picnic today regardless of the weather. Horace woke up early and packed the basket. Agnes is usually in charge of the food, so she is a little dubious of Horace's possible choices.

"Did you bring grapes?"

"Yes Agnes, I brought grapes."

"Did you wash them?"

"Yes Agnes, I washed them and I
also brought wine."

"Did you remember the wine
opener?"

"Agnes my love, it's your job to
find us the perfect spot and my
job to provide
the perfect picnic, which I
did . . . I even packed the ants."

PICNIC

Horace can get so wrapped up in his bird books that he misses signs. Agnes has been flirting madly to no avail. Exasperated, she gives him a playful swat and takes off running. Horace knows this game. He drops his book and takes off after her. They are laughing and running crazily through an open field. Anyone watching this race can plainly see that Agnes is a lot faster than Horace. She has to slow down at the end so he can catch her. She's playing hard to get, but not that hard.

HARD TO GET

Horace and Agnes go out almost every weekend but sometimes Agnes puts on her "stay-at-home-dress" to signal they're in for the night. Her quilted Asian-style ensemble is strictly used for lounging and occasional hair dyeing. Horace doesn't mind staying in. He's content to lean up against Agnes and peruse his record collection. The phone rings and Agnes starts chattering away under the hair dryer. Horace thinks it's one of her girlfriends and that she'll be on the phone for hours, but she's off in a flash. "Who was that?" Horace asks.

*"Your lovely neighbor Irene,"* Agnes says with a fake
  *smile.*
*"What does Ms. Klench want this time?"*
*"You left the trash cans out too long this week,"* Agnes
  *shouts from underneath her hair dryer.*
*Horace grimaces. "I can't believe you're nice to that*
  *pill."*
*"Horace my love, we all know you get more flies with*
  *honey, and we get fewer calls from Irene when you*
  *bring the trash cans in on time."*

STAY-AT-HOME DRESS

eering over her steering wheel, Irene Klench surveys the neighborhood. "Ohh, Mr. Freeman, you shouldn't be watering your lawn during the shortage," she says to herself as she jots down the infraction in her little black book. Irene heads out early in the mornings with a thermos full of Chock full o'Nuts and an old pair of binoculars. There is no stopping Irene when she's on her fifth cup. Once she tried to make a citizen's arrest on Horace when he was crossing the street. "It's called jaywalking!" Irene shouts from her car window. "It's called a crosswalk, Ms. Klench!" Horace shouts back as he hurries across the street. "Oh, sorry, Horace," Irene says, slightly embarrassed. "I didn't recognize you in your new jacket. I will call and get this crosswalk freshly painted tomorrow. It's barely visible," she admits before lurching off in her old car. Irene takes the neighborhood watch very seriously. Nobody is above the law. Not even her.

IRENE KLENCH

# Friendship

· · · · · · · · · · · · · · · · · · · · · ·

Agnes's oldest friend, Bertie, likes to drop in unannounced, and it's usually around mealtime. Bertie always has the latest gossip and follows up each story with "But don't tell anyone." Horace mostly plays bystander when the ladies are in their element, though he does notice that no matter how much food is on the table, Bertie's fork always wanders over to his plate. He's tried to address this with Agnes, but she just smiles sweetly and says, "Oh, Horace, friends have flaws . . . Eat faster next time."

Agnes darling, I am soooo bored. You need to throw a fabulous dinner party. I'll help—I promise." Agnes knows that Bertie has no intention of helping. Bertie is fun-loving but easily distracted, especially by shiny things. Her favorite shiny thing is the diamond from her ex-husband. She insists that her ring looks a lot better than the secretary he ran off with. "Just because it's younger doesn't mean it works better," Bertie quips as she flicks her wrist in the air. "But you know, Agnes, I wish them all the best." Agnes knows all right . . . she knows it's time to pour Bertie another glass of wine and start planning that party.

millie and Minnie Humphrey have lived together for years in a tiny apartment above their craft shop, aptly named Bits 'n Bows. They specialize in scrapbooking and decoupage. The sisters tend to bicker with each other, but they are tremendously kind to others. Millie stirs her tea quietly but then suddenly pipes up, "As you can see, we are NOT identical. Minnie has a much bigger head." Minnie laughs out loud, saying, "If my head is so big, how come you're wearing my hat!" They both ponder this fact for a moment and then simultaneously reach for the last biscuit. "Minnie dear, can you fetch some more of those delicious biscuits you baked?" Minnie hoists herself off her chair and heads into the kitchen. "Certainly Mill, but try to refrain from flattery . . . I wouldn't want my head to get any bigger."

marietta is an editor at *Audubon* magazine and has been researching migration habits and murmurations. Horace had written her a letter telling her how much he enjoyed her articles, and they started up a correspondence. Now she, Horace, and Agnes are all great friends and go on birding expeditions together. Agnes is intrigued by how far Marietta can turn her head. She never misses a thing. Marietta says very matter-of-factly, "Agnes, it just comes naturally. I've always been a keen observer. It's how I live my life. Stay quiet and alert . . . and don't let anything ruffle your feathers."

MARIETTA WEISS

Dolly was born and raised in the UK and studied art in the salons of Paris. She came to America after a scandalous affair with a married French aristocrat left her heartbroken. Dolly is much happier now with her newfound bucolic life. She's a prolific painter and shows her work regularly but prefers to be somewhat reclusive. Agnes has tried numerous times to set her up on dates, but Dolly is resolved to being alone. "Oh, Agnes, you know there was only one man for me." Agnes wishes there was something she could do, but it seems that ship has sailed. *Quel dommage . . .*

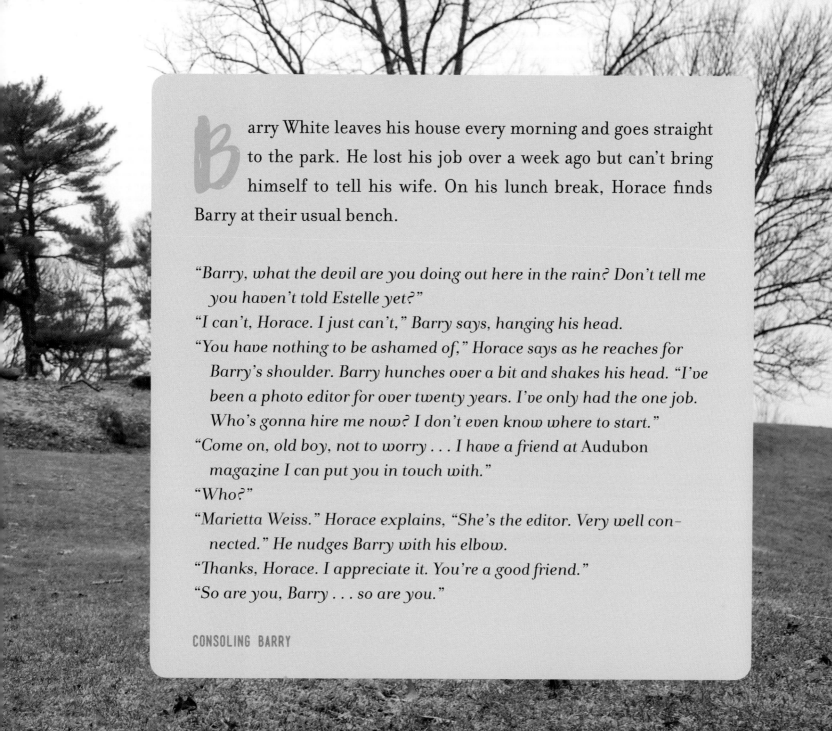

**B**arry White leaves his house every morning and goes straight to the park. He lost his job over a week ago but can't bring himself to tell his wife. On his lunch break, Horace finds Barry at their usual bench.

*"Barry, what the devil are you doing out here in the rain? Don't tell me you haven't told Estelle yet?"*

*"I can't, Horace. I just can't," Barry says, hanging his head.*

*"You have nothing to be ashamed of," Horace says as he reaches for Barry's shoulder. Barry hunches over a bit and shakes his head. "I've been a photo editor for over twenty years. I've only had the one job. Who's gonna hire me now? I don't even know where to start."*

*"Come on, old boy, not to worry . . . I have a friend at Audubon magazine I can put you in touch with."*

*"Who?"*

*"Marietta Weiss." Horace explains, "She's the editor. Very well con-nected." He nudges Barry with his elbow.*

*"Thanks, Horace. I appreciate it. You're a good friend."*

*"So are you, Barry . . . so are you."*

CONSOLING BARRY

# Available Bachelors

·····················

Downtown at the federal courthouse there is a stenotype operator named Ferris Twig. He has witnessed many high-profile cases in his eight-year tenure. He's obsessed with mob-related cases such as racketeering and extortion—he just can't get enough. His hope is to one day write a bestselling crime novel. Every Thursday during his lunch break Ferris races to the theater to catch the matinees. Currently playing is *Taxi* with James Cagney. From the dark, empty theater all you can hear is the faint nibbling of popcorn and Ferris mouthing out every word.

FERRIS TWIG

By the time I'm finished with garbage, it's squeaky clean and green," says Bill Beatty, the new head of recycling at the waste management plant. Bill went to school with Horace and they still hang out once a week for gentlemen's poker. On the remaining nights, Bill cavorts with all types of women. He's a fixture at most of the local clubs. Bill admits he's a bit of a player but insists there's nothing wrong with it. "Variety is the spice of life," he says as he eyeballs the waitress bringing him another cognac. "But I do try to stay away from drama. I have three simple rules: no crazies, no husbands, and no kids."

WILLIAM BEATTY

ick Peck is an old family friend of Agnes's. He grew up wealthy, but has never really found his calling. His recent foray into politics hasn't been easy. Dick just has a habit of saying the wrong thing. Horace has tried to help him with his campaign—he even took his photo, but Dick is resistant to constructive criticism. "I think I know what's best, Horace, but thanks for your suggestion. Hey, take a bumper sticker, will you . . . I just got them printed." Horace grimaces at the stack and chooses the least offensive one. "Vote Dick-Less Government." Then he laughs to himself because he's going to put it on Agnes's car anyway.

RICHARD PECK

Phillip J. Weber aka Flip is a high school music teacher. He'll tell you the J stands for Jazz, but it really stands for Jerome. Flip met Agnes when they taught school together. She was passing the music room while Flip was playing the piano, and she just stuck her head in and started singing. He was playing "Don't Get Around Much Anymore," which is one of Agnes's favorites. Then Flip broke out his old jazz collection and they had a discussion over the merits of Fats Waller. Flip really got a kick out of how knowledgeable she was. He just loved to egg Agnes on during the school day. Every time he'd pass her in the hall he'd shout out, "Are you keeping it cool, Agnes?" and in return, she would casually glide past him and nod: "I'm hip, Flip."

FLIP WEBER

ertie is forty-two minutes late. "I'm so sorry, darling," Bertie says as she tosses her handbag on the sofa and pulls a chair to the table. "I got caught up shopping at Gimbels and you'll NEVER guess who I ran into." Agnes attempts to, but before she can get a word out, Bertie runs right over her. "Grace! Grace Spotsfield! Can you believe it?!" Agnes can't believe it. "She's been in Switzerland. She's been gone for almost a year and now she's back," Bertie says with elation. She is so pleased that there's another divorcée in the neighborhood besides her. "It was a hideous affair, but Grace came out all right, didn't she?" Agnes just nods. "I bet she had to open a Swiss bank account with all that cash she landed," Bertie howls, slapping her hand down on the table. Then she throws both hands in the air. "Darling!" she shouts. "You HAVE to invite her to Horace's birthday party!" Agnes opens her mouth to respond but Bertie cuts her off again. "I'll call her for you to let her know."

TEA WITH BERTIE

# Horace's Birthday

· · · · · · · · · · · · · · · ·

BIRTHDAY BOY

ow was Switzerland, Grace?" Horace asks while he shakes up a Sidecar. "Did you get a chance to hit the slopes?" "Why yes, Horace, I did. I spent a few months in Saint Moritz, where I had the MOST charming ski instructor," says Grace, with a dreamy look in her eye. Bertie twists her ring around her finger as she jealously listens in. "You know, Grace, I have a friend here tonight I think you might like," Horace says, giving her a big wink. "Do tell, Horace," Grace says excitedly. Bertie continues to fidget. This is not working out the way she planned. Grace was supposed to be her ally, not her competition. She blames Horace, of course, for fawning all over her. "Sven Wreckiavik," he says, gesturing across the room. "You can't miss him. He's the one in the wheelchair. He's a bit of an adventurist, shall we say . . . Fell off a mountain last week, but he's a quick healer." A very handsome Sven sees Horace pointing and starts to wheel over. Bertie grumbles into her drink, "Yeah, Grace, if you're nice maybe he'll ask you to dance."

THE DIVORCÉES

Before Sven can even wheel across the room, Ken Holstein sidles up to Grace.

"Hey doll, I haven't seen you around here. Are you new in town?"

Sven, sensing his opportunity is in jeopardy, drives his wheelchair full-bore into the couple and conveniently runs over Ken's toe. "Ahh!" Ken groans as he grips the handles of the rogue chair. Sven immediately grabs his neck with both hands and lets out a soft little hiss. Grace leans in, concerned. "Oh my! Are you okay?" Sven smiles and assures her he's fine. Introductions are made all around, and the three chat about Sven's misadventures on his last climb. "Oh, I told him to cut the rope . . . It was the only way." Ken and Grace seem to be equally riveted. The Humphrey sisters have been listening in as well. Minnie has been relaying the whole conversation to Millie, who is just out of earshot. "So what do you think, Mill?" Millie delicately sips her tea. "My money's on Sven."

Horace's lawyer, Kit Morris, has joined the party. She brought her colleague Ken Holstein, but it seems he's run off in another direction. Kit's a remarkable litigator but her true passion is writing. She's already published a few romance novels under the name Coretta Foxx. They are VERY steamy. "I enjoyed your last book, Kit," Marietta says. "I read it from a duck blind while doing research," she says without blinking. "Kept me warm . . ." Ferris Twig, now caught in the middle of girl talk, has turned purple with embarrassment. Marietta continues regardless. "The interrogation room chapter was quite something. Do you write from experience?" Kit unwittingly rests her hand on Ferris. "Oh, Marietta, I'll have to plead the fifth on that one!"

KIT MORRIS

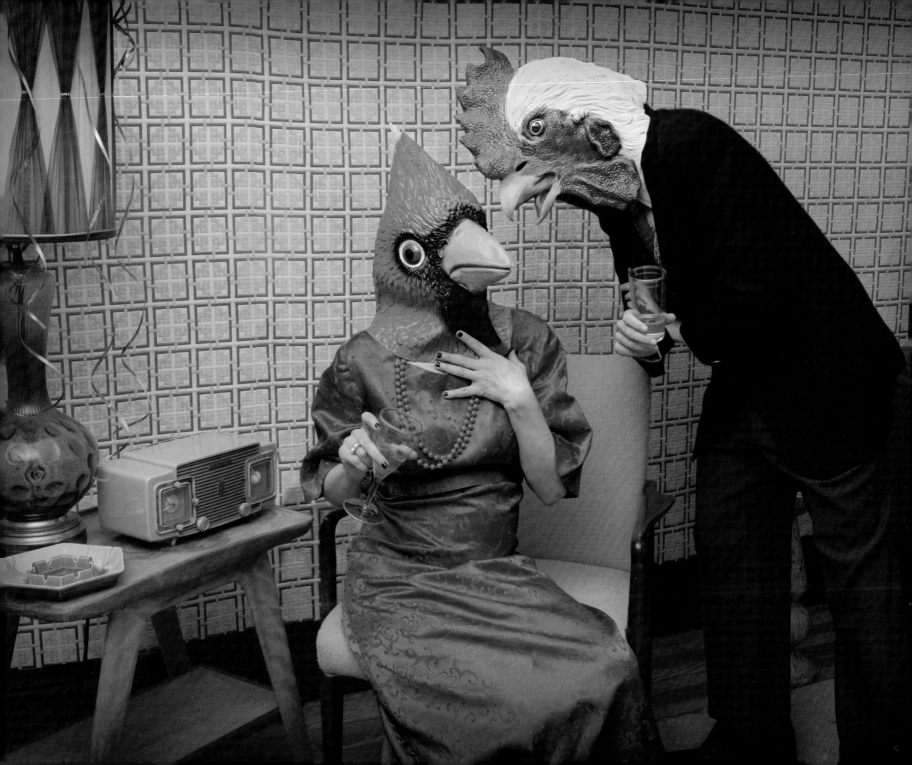

Councilman Dick Peck has brought a date to Horace's birthday party. Dick introduces his new love, Scarlet Bushelle, to Horace. "So nice to make your acquaintance," Scarlet says in a surprising baritone. She reaches out and crushes Horace's hand with her forceful grip. Dick starts to spout off about how Scarlet's in showbiz. "She's an AMAZING singer and she does great impressions." Horace smiles politely and excuses himself to help Agnes in the kitchen.

*"Agnes, I think your friend Dick is dating a man."*
*"Oh, how lovely," Agnes says, popping hors d'oeuvres in the oven.*
*"No, darling, I mean to tell you, I don't think Dick knows it's a man." Agnes peers around the corner and spies Scarlet passing by in her long blue gown.*
*"Well, that could be"—Agnes pauses—"but that dress is gorgeous."*
*"Are you going to tell him?" Horace asks anxiously.*
*"No, darling, and neither are you. Let's just leave well enough alone. Life is full of little surprises."*

After cake, Horace takes advantage of his captive audience. "Anyone wanna see our home movies?" he asks rhetorically as he plugs in the projector. The Humphrey twins clap their hands together playfully, while Bill Beatty volunteers to get the lights for his own purposes. A faint "Oh, brother" is heard from Ken Holstein, who has obviously had too much to drink. "This is Agnes and me at Lake Meade," Horace says proudly. Agnes squeezes his arm, remembering all the great times they had there. "It looks dreadfully hot," Millie says, wiping her brow. Minnie nods as she stuffs more chocolate in her mouth. The footage is inspiring Kit. "Desert heat," she mumbles. Meanwhile, more than a few guests have made it past inspiration. Dick and Scarlet are officially canoodling, Grace has her hand on Sven's knee, and Bill has dropped his arm around Bertie. The rest of the back row, resembling birds on a wire, are keeping to themselves. Marietta, who's been observing the whole scene with her extraordinary night vision, says in an audible tone, "Who needs romance novels when you can watch a home movie?"

# Road Trip

· · · · · · · · · · ·

One. Two. Three. Four suitcases. They are going away for only a few days, but Agnes keeps packing. Horace can feel his back spasm with each new bag she puts out. Traveling with Agnes usually means a full carload, and just when Horace thinks he's done, she finds something else that needs to be crammed in. "Agnes, really . . . do you have to bring your hair dryer?"

TRAVELS WITH AGNES

*"Horace, please. Beauty
doesn't happen by itself!"*

HORACE IS READY

Horace and Agnes were looking to get an early start after their motel stay in Pleasant Valley, but Agnes is still poking around the room. When she finally emerges, he curiously asks her what she's been up to. "I've been making the bed and tidying up the room, of course," she answers. Horace looks up and says, "Dear, I think they have people to do that." Agnes reaches back and closes the door behind her. "I know, Horace, but I don't want them to think we are pigs."

PLEASANT VALLEY

On their road trip, Horace reads the maps and Agnes drives. Horace is a very detailed navigator and Agnes has a lead foot. By Horace's calculations they are right near one of their favorite spots, the Beaver Den Diner, so they stop for lunch. Agnes enjoys a healthy tuna sandwich, while Horace inhales a plate of fries and a milk shake. Agnes knows his sensitive stomach might not be able to handle it, but it's vacation: Let him eat cake!

It's a brilliant Chicago morning, and Agnes has commandeered Horace's 8mm movie camera to document their trip. As Horace is dryly regaling Agnes with his knowledge of the marine life in Lake Michigan, a naked man in a tricolored wig streaks past, followed by three police officers. They are both quite astounded. Horace leans in, barely moving his lips: "Agnes, please tell me you got that." She leans back into him, and says, "Don't worry, dear, it's in the can."

TELL ME YOU GOT THAT

Horace likes to surprise Agnes with little weekend getaways. He tries to find small motels on the shoreline so they can both get their feet wet. They bird-watch, collect shells, and take as many snapshots as film allows. Horace likes to say they are making memories with every click.

L ook, Agnes," Horace says as he gently puts a sand dollar in the palm of her hand, "I found another one."

*"Oh, Horace, it's as perfect as the last one."*
*"I'm going to get you one for every year we've been married."*
*"Dear, there's no need to empty the ocean for me . . . we have plenty."*
*Horace surveys the rolling waves. "You know . . . there's plenty of fish in the sea, but I caught myself a real marlin," he says, wrapping his arm around Agnes.*
*"I'll just have to assume that's a compliment, Horace"—she brushes the sand from her hands— "but you certainly knew how to hook me."*

I FOUND THIS FOR YOU

# Time Apart

· · · · · · · · · · · · · · · · ·

Every year Agnes heads off to Delaware for a week to visit her sister Flora. They are quite different in looks and personality, but they both enjoy good fun. The amusement park down the street is usually their first stop. Agnes misses Horace already, but she thinks it's good to get away once in a while—it makes you appreciate what you have. Horace concurs. He always tells her on her way out the door: "Absence makes me handsomer."

THREE CHEERS MOTEL

now that Agnes is away, Horace is happy to break all of the house rules. Agnes runs a tight ship, so she would be horrified to know that he was eating in their bed. But as Horace sees it, he's got seven whole days to change the sheets and no one is the wiser.

oor Agnes loves pets, but she is so allergic to them that she has to settle for porcelain ones. The poodles, Fifi and Prince, are from Agnes's grandmother's house, and Horace found Daffodil the cat at a yard sale. Horace is not a fan of the poodles, but he adores the cat. What's more, he likes to say, "If Agnes is happy, I'm happy . . . and how can you go wrong for fifty cents?"

Horace is probably the only guy who doesn't mind TV dinners. He especially likes the odd texture of what is supposed to be corn. They ring each other almost every day but it's Agnes's turn to call tonight, so he's moved the phone near the television so he won't have to get up while watching an episode of *Ironside*. Of course, it doesn't really matter where Horace puts the phone; if Agnes calls, he'll come running.

"Hi, Horace," Agnes says sweetly.

"How did you know it was me?" chirps the phone's receiver.

"Darling, I just know," Agnes says confidently. "You're calling awfully early. How have you been faring without me?"

"Oh, it's been easy enough, the dancing girls just left. How about you?"

"Just ogling all the brawny lifeguards," Agnes says casually.

"Hmm"—Horace considers—"I didn't think they were your type."

"True enough," says Agnes. "I guess I'm more partial to amusing intellectuals."

"I know someone like that," Horace says cheerfully.

Agnes laughs. "I'm sure you do."

"Well"—Horace pauses—"I'll let you get back to your sister. I just wanted to hear your voice. Bonsoir, my dove."

"Arrivederci, Muscles."

Agnes loves to read, day or night. She's already finished several books while she's been away. She thinks of Horace as she giggles through a lurid love scene and remembers how, when he decides the lights have been on too long, he will wrestle a book away from her and begin a dramatic reading from the last page. She's not the least bit bothered. As she'll tell anyone over tea, "Horace has had some Oscar-winning performances."

MURDER IN A NUNNERY

Horace was all ready for bed when he heard a knock at the door. When he opened it, he couldn't believe his eyes: It was Agnes! "I took an early train," she said. Horace didn't even wait for her to put down her bag. "I've missed you so much," he said as he grabbed her for a hug. Agnes was so exhausted that all she wanted to do was go straight to bed. As they snuggled in together, Agnes leaned over to Horace and whispered, "Have you been eating in this bed?" Horace quickly propped himself up on his pillow and replied, "Why would you ask me that?" Agnes put his face in her hands and grinned: "Because these sheets are clean."

LATE-NIGHT SURPRISE

# Long Hot Summer

CITY HARBOR

Agnes, get a load of that guy over there. What in the world . . ." Horace is dispatching running commentary as they wait for the 424 bus. Agnes is exhausted after a full day of sightseeing and can't wait to get off her feet.

*"Horace dear, don't be unkind."*

*"C'mon, Agnes," Horace moans. "The best part of coming to the city is people-watching."*

*"That's true, sweetheart, but don't forget, they're looking at you, too."*

*"What's wrong with me?" Horace asks plainly.*

*"Luckily nothing . . . because I pick out all your clothes," Agnes says nonchalantly while peering out for the bus.*

*Horace laughs out loud. "Very well, I will be good." Just as he declares silence, a lady walks by who looks just like Ernest Borgnine.*

PEOPLE - WATCHING

orace and Agnes have invited Bill Beatty and Bertie Swopes over to watch the town fireworks. Bertie seems unusually toxic, which prompts Horace to interrogate Bill. "What the heck is going on with you two?" Horace murmurs under his breath as he shakes the remaining ice cubes in his glass. "Are you dating?"

*"I wouldn't call it dating," Bill says, lifting his eyebrow and crossing his legs.*

*"Listen, Beatty, don't muck around with Agnes's friend. You are chaos incarnate."*

*"Worry not, my high-strung pal, I've got it all under control." Bill stands up and offers a toast. "Happy Fourth, everyone!" Unfortunately only three glasses go up. There're definitely going to be fireworks tonight.*

"Minnie, don't let go of me."

"Oh, Millie, you have two floaty rings. What could possibly happen to you?"

"Minnie, you shouldn't even be in the water . . . you just ate," Millie says authoritatively.

"Millie! I had that cream puff over twenty minutes ago . . . But I guess if you'd like me to leave you here all alone, I'd be happy to."

"Minnie, don't be rash," her sister says in an agitated voice. "I didn't realize it had been THAT long since you ate." Their bickering is drowned out by the sound of Bill Beatty heading down to shore.

"Anyone here available to put some suntan lotion on my back!" he shouts. A small tidal surge hits the beach as Minnie and Millie storm out of the water. Minnie wins hands down, as Millie has become entangled in her flotation devices. This time at least, it seems that two tubes are too many.

INNER TUBES

Horace can float, but he isn't as comfortable in the water as Agnes is. She grew up on the ocean and has been swimming her whole life. He thinks she could grow gills by the amount of time she spends in the water. He's confident to paddle about, knowing that Agnes is nearby. If he starts to go under, she can always save him without missing a stroke.

LIFESAVER

gnes stands in a sea of dandelions searching for her Horace. She can barely see him along the edge of the field. "Horace!" she shouts, waving her hat back and forth. Horace tips his hat and heads toward her. The last thing she remembers is dozing off in Horace's lap. The sun was deliciously hot outside their flowered patio umbrella. As Horace approaches, he holds out his cupped hands.

*"Strawberries, my dear, wild strawberries!" he exclaims.*
*"Well done, my love, you found us dessert. But how did you ever get up without waking me?"*
*"Wake you? You were out cold. I think you were snoring." He laughs out loud.*
*"Horace! I was not!" Agnes says and whacks him with her hat.*
*"Would it help if I said you're adorable when you snore?"*
*Agnes takes a strawberry from his hand. "I do not snore, mister."*
*"Okay, missus"—Horace rolls his eyes—"then you're just adorable."*

DANDELION FIELD

# Catching Up with Family

· · · · · · · · · · · · · · · · · · · · · ·

Horace and Agnes are in California to visit his estranged sister Felicity. Instead of meeting up right away, Agnes has planned a relaxing drive down the coast to help Horace unwind. They stop at almost every ocean overlook to get a glimpse of the seals and the surfers. "Don't you think that would be fun, Horace?" Agnes asks, pointing to a group of young surfers paddling out. Horace pales at the thought of being among the waves with his limited swimming skills. "I think I'll pass, but I would enjoy watching you hang ten," he snickers. Even though Agnes is tall, she is always trying to get the best view. "Horace, lift me up, darling. I think this rock will be the perfect vantage point." Horace is happy to give her a boost. He smiles to himself and thinks, From my vantage point, I have a better view.

A BETTER VIEW

Horace's sister Felicity has always been the black sheep of the family. She ran away from home at a young age, joined a commune, and renamed herself Crystal. She led a wild life, which included hard drugs and petty crime. There was also a very long line of unsavory suitors. After all these years she has finally gotten her life back together. Crystal found new love with her tango instructor, Miguel, and is studying at night to be a yoga instructor. Horace knows she's still untamed, but is happy that she's found a healthier path. Agnes and Felicity have never met before and Horace has yet to meet Miguel. It should make for an interesting weekend.

CRYSTAL GROOMSBY AND MIGUEL

Agnes and Crystal have really connected. They have been talking nonstop. Horace hasn't been so lucky with Miguel, whom he's renamed Biceps. Miguel has a rough touch and has taken to punching Horace in the arm as a sentence finisher. Miguel is insistent that everyone get in the pool since he's turned up the heat, but Horace has no intention of swimming unless he absolutely has to. He is content to sit in his lounge chair and listen to the ladies. They are currently dissecting his childhood. He hopes by lunch they make it past puberty.

Agnes has arranged a quick trip to Los Angeles before they leave California. She insists that they close out their tour with a visit to the museum. Horace can't complain; he's dragged her all over Hollywood to see every kitschy relic. While standing in the lit colonnade, Horace takes note of the setting sun and pops down on one knee. "Agnes, my darling . . . I propose"—he pauses—"that we go to Pink's tomorrow for hot dogs." Agnes swoons. "Oh, Horace, I can't wait to sit in traffic and stand in a really long line for a hot dog." Onlookers snap a few photos as they think something else is going on. "Okay, Romeo, on your feet," Agnes says, holding her arm out. Horace jumps back up and slings his arm around her. "I'd marry you all over again, Doll Face." Agnes rests her head on Horace's shoulder as they stroll back down the colonnade. She loves when he calls her Doll Face.

PROPOSAL

# Out West

· · · · · · · · · · · · · · · · · ·

Equipped with a fistful of brochures from his sister, Horace persuades Agnes to spend some time in nature out West. They amble their way through the desert, stopping at whatever catches their fancy. Agnes pulls the car over so Horace can investigate a small outcropping of Joshua trees.

*"This heat's gonna take some getting used to," Horace says, tugging at his polyester collar. "Do you think we look like city slickers out here?"*

*Agnes glances at his shirt with a zebra on it. "Well, we certainly don't look local."*

*"Then I need to get a cowboy hat," Horace says definitively.*

*"Yes, sweetheart . . ." Agnes says, shading her eyes, "that should do it."*

*Horace continues to stare ahead, admiring the vast terrain and her gentle sarcasm. "Just you wait, my dear . . . there's gonna be a new sheriff in town.*

POLYESTER DESERT

HOWDY MA'AM

**m**y God, Agnes, come look at this," Horace says, admiring the trees. Agnes heads over from the car barefoot with her shoes in her hands.

"Oh, Horace, the yellow is so vibrant." As the wind picks up, the trees start to sway. "The trees are dancing," she says admiringly. Not to be outdone by the foliage, Horace scoops up Agnes and begins his version of a waltz.

"Horace, you're crazy. There isn't even any music."

"Well then, you'd better start singing," he says.

When Horace goes in for the big dip, he accidentally slips and sends them both to the ground in a heap. Agnes laughs hysterically as he helps her to her feet. Horace chuckles, too, saying, "I guess I need more classes at Arthur Murray, or at the very least, a trip to the gym."

DANCING TREES

Agnes dear, can you pull over soon? I'd like to get some water out of the trunk." It's been a long drive through Death Valley and Horace is a bit parched. At the next stop, Horace fishes out his thermos, and by the time he's done, he spies Agnes wandering off through the brush. He follows suit and, seemingly out of nowhere, they both come across a sea of palm trees. "It's an oasis!" she exclaims. Horace slowly removes his hat. "Agnes, it's a hundred five degrees. If this is an oasis, I know why they call it Death Valley."

THE PALMS

WELCOME TO LAS VEGAS

MOTEL
Holiday
MOTEL
WELCOME
POOL, COFFEE
MAJORC REDIT CARDS
FAMILY ROOMS
CABLE TV
VACANCY
pepsi

Before they check into their motel room, Agnes reminds Horace of what happened the last time they came to Vegas. Apparently Horace lost a lot of money at the craps table, thinking he knew how to play better than he did, and he didn't own up to it until they got home.

*"Agnes, it won't be like last time. I've been studying up."*
*"Horace, it's not about studying, it's about setting limits."*
*"I know, I know . . . I'm only going to play the five-dollar table, and if I'm still losing after an hour, I'm going to walk away."*
*Agnes lets out a big sigh, "Darling, all I'm saying is, don't roll the dice with me."*

LOW ROLLER

Horace and Agnes emerge from the casino doors eight hundred dollars richer.

*"Oh, Horace, that was so exciting," Agnes says, beaming as they queue in the taxi stand. They spent nearly two hours playing craps before the table got hot. A string of sevens turned Horace's meager stack of chips into three healthy columns. Attempting to roll a "hard ten," Horace shook the dice in his fist, held them up for Agnes to blow on, and sent them down the felt. "HAARD TEN!" the croupier yelled, and the table erupted in cheers. Horace quickly cashed out and finally left a winner. A taxi pulls up and they both hop in.*

*"My good man, who has the best clams casino in town?"*

*The cabbie suggests the Golden Steer. "Well, that's settled, then," Horace says, and hands the man an early tip. "Steer us to the Steer!"*

RED ROCK CANYON

Hey mister! How much to rent the Hudson?" Horace has his eye on a beautiful turquoise vintage car. Agnes is just as keen. Her father used to have one just like it. Horace wheels and deals and gets the rental for a song. He opens the door for Agnes and tips his hat. "Your chariot, my dear." She climbs in while Horace runs around to the other side. Then he revs the engine and leans in toward Agnes and asks, "Ready for vintage driving vintage?" She sweeps her scarf around her head and laughs. "Speak for yourself, Horace—I'm a spring chicken."

VINTAGE RENTAL

ell, so much for nostalgia," Horace groans as he gets out of the now-defunct Hudson. Steam pours from the hood, and a very irritated Agnes plunks herself down on her suitcase on the side of the road. Horace opens the hood and gives it a manly look over before declaring he has no idea what's wrong. Agnes looks up at him and solemnly states that the vacation is now ruined. Horace assures Agnes that he will take care of everything and not to worry. Then he assumes the traditional hitchhiking stance. He can see that she's distressed, so he breaks into some fancy dance moves with his thumb out. It looks like a cross between an umpire and a traffic cop doing the Charleston. Agnes tries not to laugh, but eventually she can't help herself. "Oh, Horace, if you keep acting like a nut, we'll never get picked up."

IT'S ALL RUINED

H orace, did you see that bullet hole in the elevator?" Agnes asks. "Do you think it's real?" Horace smiles and crinkles his paper. "Darling, we are in the Wild West. Of course it's real." Agnes ponders for a moment while staring into the mirror. "I can't imagine what it was like back then, so rough and tumble. You'd be working all day in the silver mines and I'd be living out of a tent!" "Hah! I'd be the one in a tent. You'd be back East with your parents. Of course I would send for you when I struck it rich," Horace says, without looking up from his paper. "Hey . . . listen to this. It says that a lady of the evening had a deadly run-in with a jealous suitor in the early 1900s. It ended badly for her on the fifth floor and now she haunts the hotel."

*"Oh, Horace, how awful. The poor dear!" Agnes says. "I'm glad you didn't*
  *tell me that last night—I wouldn't have slept a wink."*
*"Indeed," Horace sighs, "no silver lining for her."*

A gnes, did you know there are thirteen different kinds of rattlesnakes in Arizona?" Agnes quickly recoils as if she's about to step on one.

"What in the world made you bring that up, Horace?"

"Nothing." Horace shrugs. "Just thought you'd like to know. The diamondback is responsible for most of the bites," he says as he kicks a stone into the shrubs.

"Well, now that you've got me sufficiently terrified, I'd like to go back to the car," Agnes says, turning around.

"Oh, Agnes, they won't be out this time of day," he says confidently. Agnes lets out a big sigh and grabs Horace's arm. Just as she latches on, the shrub starts to rattle. Both Horace and Agnes take off in a full sprint back to the car. As Horace pants heavily, he reaches for Agnes and puts his arm around her.

"I'm glad I was there to protect you."

"Yes, Horace. It was very gentlemanly of you to let me get to the car first."

RATTLESNAKE

WAITING FOR SUNSET

"Agnes, can we stop for a minute?" Horace wobbles. "I don't feel well." Agnes spins around just in time to catch Horace falling forward. "Darling, why aren't you wearing your hat . . . and why are you still wearing your sport coat?"

*"I like to look nice for you," Horace says, wiping his brow.*
*"Sweetheart! Don't be ridiculous. . . ." Agnes digs deep into her bottomless bag of everything and pulls out a bottle of water. "You are dehydrated, that's all." Agnes forces liquids into Horace and sweetly rubs his forehead. "Okay, handsome, we're almost done with this trail." She turns about-face and charges down a new path. Horace puts on his hat and quickly follows her. If there's one thing he knows about desert survival, it's follow the lady with the water.*

SUN STROKE

# Autumn Turns

· · · · · · · · · · · · · ·

A gnes, do you know what's worse than finding a worm in your apple?"

"No, Horace. . . ." She waits patiently.

"Half a worm!"

Agnes giggles and bites into her freshly picked apple. She knows Horace can be a little corny. That's one of the things she loves about him. As Horace industriously piles more apples into his hat, she starts to mull over all the recipes in her head. Tarts . . . crisps . . . pies . . . crumbles. Horace glances over at Agnes, who appears to be stuck in a trance.

"I've seen that face before," he says wryly. "You've already started cooking. Looks like we better up our supply: I'm gonna need a bigger hat."

APPLE PICKING

Horace and Agnes have just checked into a beautiful old mansion that happens to be a bed-and-breakfast. Horace lugs the bags up to the fourth floor, and they both head back into town for a quiet dinner. By the time they get back, they find themselves virtually alone in the grand estate. "Horace, this dining room is exquisite," Agnes says, running her hand over the table linen. Horace pulls out a chair and plops himself down. "Have a seat, my lady," he says with a sweeping gesture. "Well, don't you sound like the lord of the manor," Agnes replies. Horace picks up a china teacup and pretends to drink out of it. "Put that down, Horace. The table is set for breakfast," Agnes chides him. Horace continues to wave the cup around. "I believe we'll have to move the regatta out a fortnight to oblige the commodore." Agnes, concerned that other guests may soon arrive, chooses to divert Horace. "The lady of the house thinks we should repair to our chambers." Horace puts the teacup down gingerly and rises from the table. "That, my dear, sounds like a capital idea."

LORD OF THE MANOR

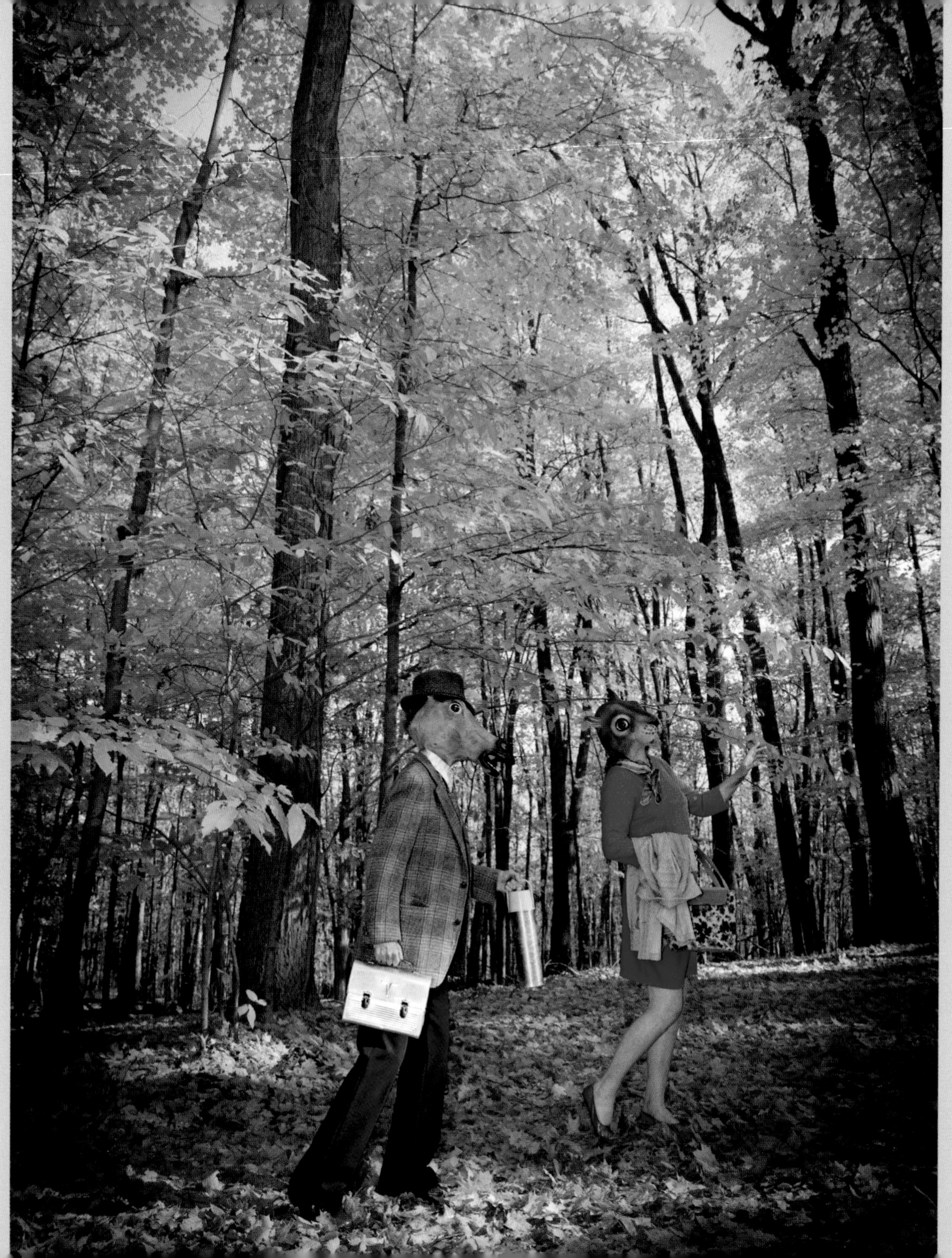

Horace and Agnes are seated in the yellow den awaiting bird-watching advice from their friend Marietta. Horace thumbs through a field manual while Agnes admires a finch replica. "Agnes, this part is incredibly interesting," Horace says as he reads the entire paragraph aloud. Agnes chooses to ignore him completely and stares at his hair instead. She's mesmerized by the way it flops back and forth when he really gets intense about something. Horace, sensing he's lost his audience, looks over the top of his glasses. "You're not even listening, are you?" Agnes admits it. Sometimes love is never having to say . . . "Stop talking."

# Days of December

· · · · · · · · · · · · · · · · · · ·

It's unusually warm for December, so Marietta Weiss has decided to squeeze in one more birding expedition with Horace before the holidays. They both stand artfully camouflaged while Marietta fiddles with the contraption slung over her shoulder. "Did you hear that?" Horace whispers loudly. Marietta gives him a mildly cross look and whispers back, "Quiet, Horace, I'm trying to record." There's a flurry of simple, sharp, high-pitched chirps coming from the thicket. She stands rigid while scanning the brush. "I think it's over there!" Horace says excitedly. Marietta glares back and puts her finger to her lips as she adjusts her headphones. "Sounds like the male orange-crowned warbler," she says with certainty. "How do you know it's a male?" Horace asks. Marietta raises her binoculars just in time to see the warbler zip off— "Because of its greenish-brown coloring and the fact that he talks too damn much."

WINTER FOWL

TOBOGGAN

It's cold and rainy out: a perfect day for a puzzle. Horace is in charge of completing the edging and arranging small piles of similar pieces for Agnes. He is in an absolute quandary because he can't finish the border. "Agnes, I've combed through this whole box. Did you hide a piece from me?" Agnes denies involvement but starts humming a little tune while she works on her section. Horace notices that the sides of her mouth are curling up. "You did take it, didn't you!" "Horace, I would never do such a thing," she says, batting her eyelids. "I'm going to have to search you, young lady," he says, pushing his chair back from the table. As he leaps up, the missing piece flies out of his pajama sleeve. "Well, that solves THAT mystery!" Agnes says triumphantly. "But I will take a rain check on that search."

LAST PIECE

It's time to do the holiday cards, so Horace and Agnes hunker down to finish them off in one fell swoop. Agnes gets out her address book and Horace retrieves the official list. He stamps and addresses all the envelopes while she gets out the typewriters. Every year Agnes crafts a long sarcastic letter spoofing their annual activities. Horace prefers to be brief in his correspondence. He types up little friendly fortunes to put in the cards. He is compelled to interrupt Agnes to read her every single one. "She who watches birds, flies right," he gleefully announces for Marietta Weiss. And for his pal Bill Beatty? "Drinking too much during poker will get you a royal flush."

There's a party at the Groomsbys': a simple affair, just Agnes's friend Bertie and the Humphrey sisters, but Agnes always has to put on the dog. After a fabulous dinner, Horace shuffles everyone into the living room and wheels out his old Victrola. Agnes gracefully sways to the music while Bertie tries her hand at the new craze The Robot. The Humphrey sisters are mirroring each other in their own made-up dance. Horace carefully brushes off Guy Lombardo's "Auld Lang Syne" and reminisces about what a great year he's had with Agnes. How did he get so lucky? he thinks. But then he turns to Agnes and says, "Do you know how lucky you are, being married to me?" Agnes reaches back while she's dancing and squeezes Horace's hand. She knows.

NEW YEAR'S EVE

3 . . . 2 . . . 1 . . . MIDNIGHT

## Endless thanks to:

Our agents, Bethany Buck and Brenda Bowen, for pitching us; at Blue Rider Press, Sarah Hochman for understanding us, and David Rosenthal for creating an eclectic net that snags oddballs like us.

Our supporters: Cami Johnson, Dar and Deborah, Jeanne Ramalho, Jadzia Kepka, Melissa and Ianko Nikolov, the Dowlings, the Stanzins, the Woodruffs, the Leonards, Nancy Hwang, Caleb Cole, Jessica Bruce, Daniel Dias, Griffin Museum of Photography, New England School of Photography, and Paul Sneyd at Panopticon Imaging.

Our cast: Cami, Kathy, Beth, Laura, Colleen, Amanda, Daphne, Jo, Angel, Susanne, Francesca, Michael C, Sophie, Kate, Barbara and Michael S, Nick, Paula and Michael P.

Our memories: Marjorie Agnes, Uncle John, Uncle Jerry, Zosia, Goshka, Jane, Nancy, and Archie.

You can't stop people from dying, but you can make the love they leave behind last a lifetime.

## About the Authors

**Lynn Dowling** is a graduate of Wheaton College and a Boston-based creative director in the design industry.

**Asia Kepka** studied set design in Lodz, Poland. A graduate of New England School of Photography, she has worked for such publications as *Wired, Fortune, Time, The New York Times Magazine*, and elsewhere. Her work has been exhibited in galleries and museums in the United States and Europe.

Dowling and Kepka live in Arlington, Massachusetts. *Horace & Agnes* is their first book.